A Silly Cat's Adirondack Adventure

DonnaInk Publications, L.L.C.

dpInk

Donnalnk Publications, L.L.C.

United States of America

Donnalnk Publications, L.L.C.
129 Daisy Hill Road, Carthage, NC 28327-7733

First Paperback Edition: November 2016. First Electronic Edition: November 2016.

Library of Congress Cataloguing in Publications Data

Beckeman, Bonnie, 2016 -
     A Silly Adirondack Cat's Adventure / by Bonnie Beckeman - 1st ed.
38 p.cm.

Summary: *A Silly Cat's Adirondack Adventure is about two cats in the Adirondacks. Maple is the main character and she is always told she can't do things like sing but she knows how to sing. Maple is a magic cat who has adventures in the Adirondacks. In this children's book Maple sings, and kayaks and communicates with frogs. This is a fun book where even the frogs and bunnies are friends of Maple. Some bunnies have wings and fly or was that a dream? Well, we all know bunnies can't fly or can they?*

~ Summary provided by Bonnie Beckeman.

ISBN: 978-1939425539 Print

[1. Literature - Fiction, 2. Juvenile Watercolor - Fiction, 3. Adirondack Children's - Fiction, 4. Fantasy - Fiction, 5. Family - Fiction, 6. Relationships - Fiction, 7. Illustration - Fiction, 8. Women's Literature – Fiction, 9. Adirondack Authors – Juvenile Fiction, 10. United States - fiction.]
     Title. II. Title: A Silly Cat's Adirondack Adventure PZ(1)-(4) [Fic]-dc23

10 9 8 7 6 5 4 3 2 1
Printed in the United States of America

A Silly Cat's Adirondack Adventure

Written & Illustrated by

Bonnie Beckeman

This Book Belongs To

Dedication . . .

This book is dedicated to
Calvin Beckeman
my only grandchild so far.

Calvin, you are the light of my life.

I hope you read this book
lots of times.

Epigraph . . .

A cat has absolute emotional honesty:
human beings, for one reason or another,
may hide their feelings, but a cat does not."

Ernest Hemingway

A Silly Cat's Adirondack Adventure

On this adventure, Maple spies Birch. He is listening to fish tell stories as they swish their tales in rhythm.

Maple dives into the Adirondack lake to catch crayfish, as the fox run!

The crayfish scuttle and hide under the rocks.

in the Adirondack lake
over their hiding places.

Calvin, the racoon, chatters to . . .

MR. BEAR

in amazement, as Maple returns to shore.

Maple PURRS
a favored Adirondack
bunny tune.

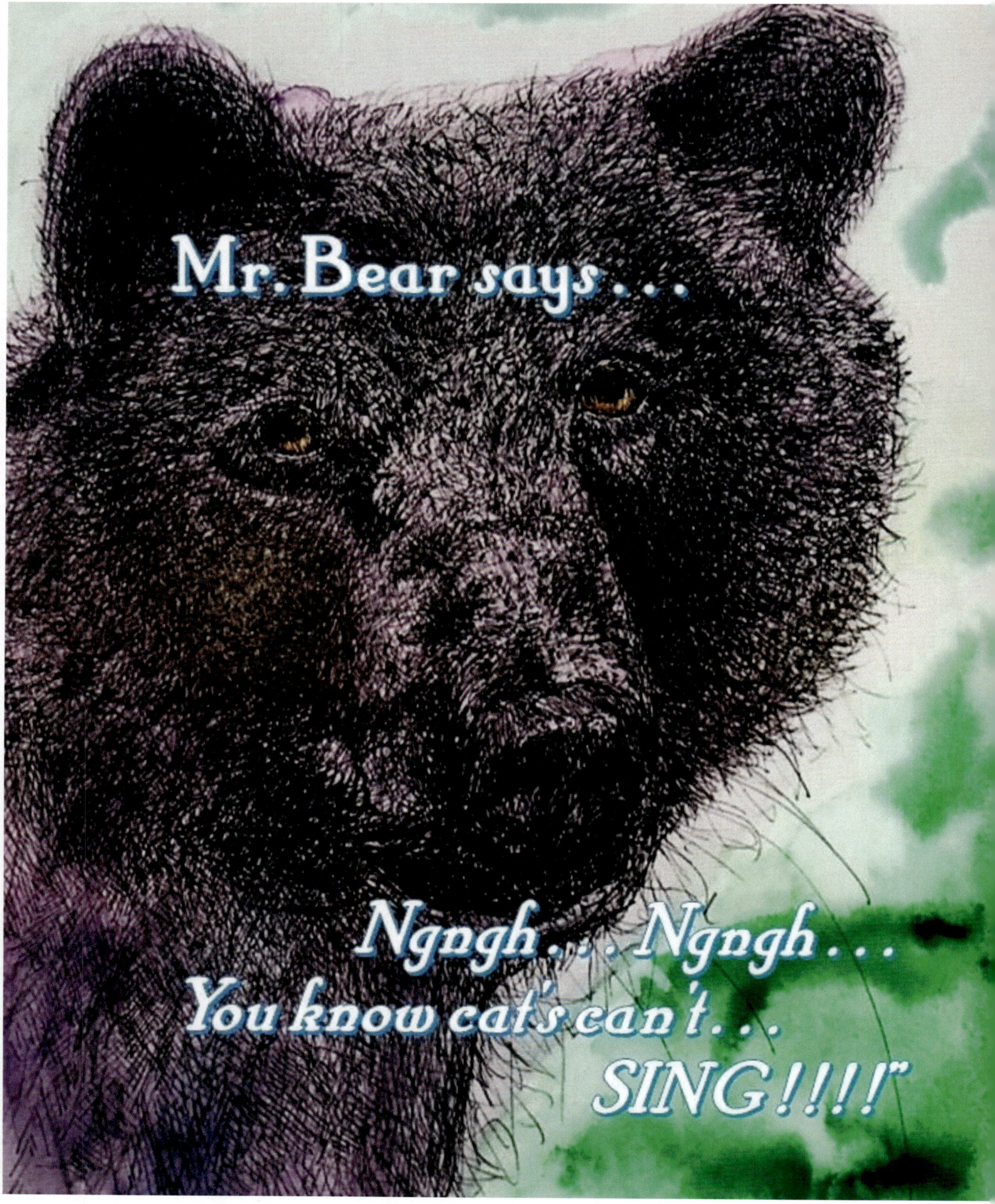
Mr. Bear says . . .
Ngngh . . . Ngngh . . .
You know cat's can't . . .
SING!!!!"

Maple & Birch
climb onto a wooden raft

to soak in the
Adirondack sunshine.

Beavers swim past with

tree branches in their mouths.

as the sun

begins its descent.

Night emerges . . . Maple is seen
kayaking by the light of the moon.
The stars shimmer on the glassy pond.
While nature's orchestra plays.

Two frogs croak their refrains
Bailing out a leaky sailboat.
Water plays on their
buckets like bongos.

They sail the evening shoreline
watching tiny minnows dart by.

"It's time to rest now." says a wise old owl.

Curling up in balsam needles,
Maple hears the lapping
Adirondack water and she
drifts into a sleepy slumber.

She dreams of bunny friends
flying in the balsam
scented mists of her
Adirondack lake.

Another Adirondack Adventure
comes to its end for Maple.
Forest creatures are
heard in the distance, saying . . .

Goodnight Maple!
Goodnight Silly Cat!

Ms. Maple . . .

the STAR of OUR Story

About the Author
And Illustrator!

Bonnie Beckeman has been drawing
since she was about six. She graduated
from New England College with a
four year degree in Art.

Bonnie studied with Ivan Powell
after college through
Syracuse University graduate department.

Ivan was one of the top ten illustrators in the nation.
Bonnie Beckeman has been painting
professionally 25 years.

She has had many amazing clients, such as
William Simon
Secretary of the Treasury
under Nixon.

Other Fine Details . . .

Websites

Author	www.wix.com/bonnie.beckeman
Publisher	www.donnaink.com

Social Media

Facebook	www.facebook.com/authorbonniebeckeman
LinkedIn	www.linkedin.com/in/bonniebeckeman
Twitter:	@AuthorBBeckeman
WordPress	authorbonniebeckeman.wordpress.com

37713341R00023

Made in the USA
Middletown, DE
04 December 2016